Amazing Grace
my chains are gone

An Easter Celebration of Worship for Congregation and Choir

Featuring the songs of
MATT REDMAN CHRIS TOMLIN
LOUIE GIGLIO STUART TOWNEND and KEITH GETTY

Created by DENNIS and NAN ALLEN
Orchestrated by DAVE WILLIAMSON

D1712737

PUBLISHING COMPANY

lillenas.com

CONTENTS IN SEQUENCE

How Can I Keep from Singing?

with

I Will Sing the Wondrous Story
I Could Sing of Your Love Forever

Words and Music by
CHRIS TOMLIN, ED CASH
and MATT REDMAN
Arr. by Dennis Allen

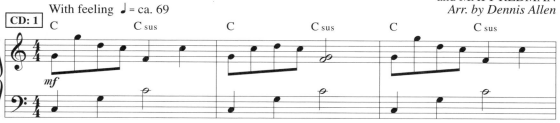

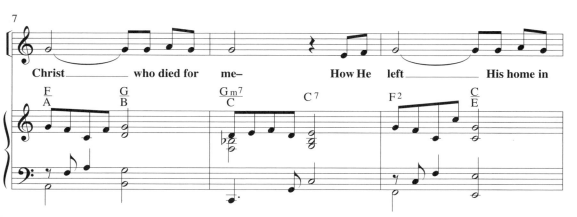

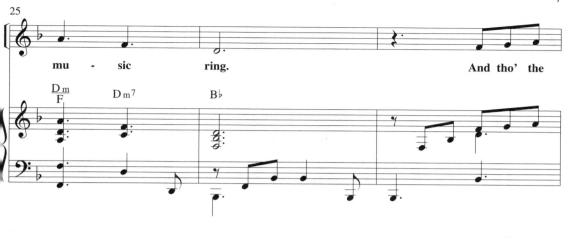

mu - sic ring. And tho' the

storms may come, I am hold - ing on,

to the Rock I cling.

8

55
LADIES *unis.*
mf

I will lift my eyes in the dark - est

F ⁴₂
dim.
F
mf
C/E

59

night, For I know my Sav - ior

C/E
Dm
Dsus/E
Dm/F
Dm⁷

62

lives! _____
mf My Sav - ior lives! And I will walk with

B♭
F

*"I Could Sing of Your Love Forever"

CHOIR *and* CONG.

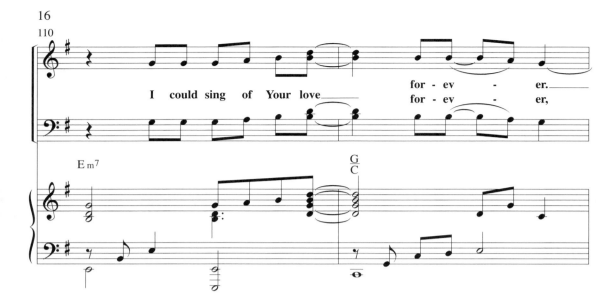

*WORSHIP LEADER: I could sing of God's love forever and ever.
I know many of you can say the same thing. Just think. One day
we'll sing together in heaven . . . for eternity . . . even after the
music stops for us here on earth. What a thought! What a blessing
to be able to say that!

Now, some of you might wonder, *(music begins)* "How can he say
that? How can he know he'll be spending eternity in heaven?"

Well, it's not by anything I have done. It's all about what Jesus did.

You Chose the Cross
(Lost in Wonder)

Words and Music by
MARTYN LAYZELL
Arr. by Dennis Allen

cresc.

O - be - di - ent___ to death___ You o - ver -
Yet not My will___ but Yours___ be done___ You

F   Cm⁷   B♭/D

came.
cried.

Parts both times
f

I'm lost in won - der,___ I'm lost in

F   B♭   F/A

love;   I'm lost in praise for - ev - er-more.___

Gm⁷   E♭M⁷

20

CD: 13

32

Opt. SOPRANOS *only*

giv - en, I am re - stored.

And

Eb M7

F

35

tho' Your soul was o - ver-whelmed with pain;

O-

C m7

Bb/D

F

37

be - di - ent to death You o - ver - came.

The

Opt. TENORS *only*

C m7

Bb/D

F

love; I'm lost in praise for - ev - er-more.

Be-cause of Je - sus'___ un - fail - ing

love; I am for - giv - en,___ I am re-stored.

51

f

I'm lost in won - der,____ I'm lost in

MEN *f*

F   B♭   F/A

f

53

love;   I'm lost in praise   for - ev - er - more.____

G m7   E♭M7

55

Be - cause of Je - sus'____ un - fail - ing

F   B♭   F/A

love; I am for - giv - en,_____ I am re -stored.

WORSHIP LEADER *(without music)*: The song says that "He loosed the cords of sinfulness. He broke the chains of our disgrace." No one else but God's Son could have done that. Though many have died for our physical freedom, only One could have died so that our souls could be free. *(Music begins)*

That One is Jesus. Sing with me about Him.

Who Is There like You?

Words and Music by
PAUL OAKLEY
Arr. by Dennis Allen

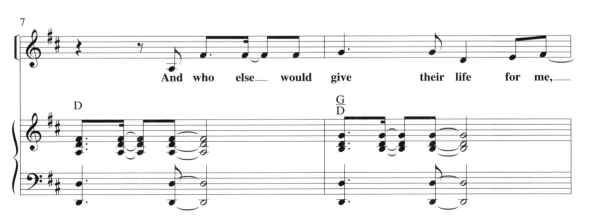

e - ven suf - fer - ing in my ___

B m7   E m7

___ place? ___   And who could re -

A sus   A 7 sus   D

pay You? ___   All of ___ cre -

G/D   D

a - tion looks to You, ___   and You pro - vide ___

G/D   B m7

WORSHIP LEADER *(without music)*: We *can* trust in His word,
His cross, His blood. *(Music begins)* Let's sing this as a testimony . . .

Nothing but the Blood

Words and Music by
ROBERT LOWRY
Arr. by Dennis Allen

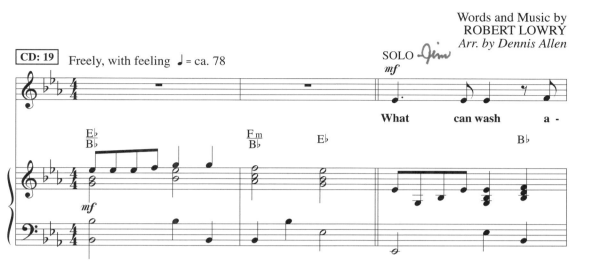

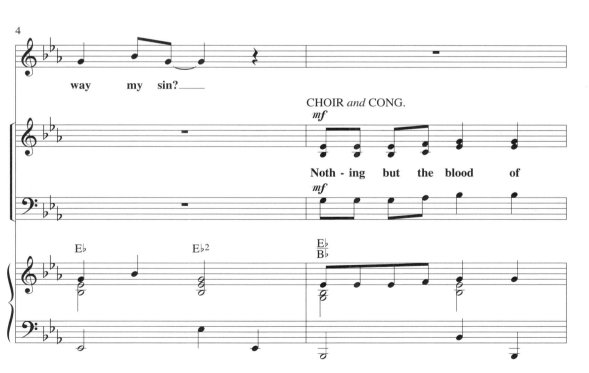

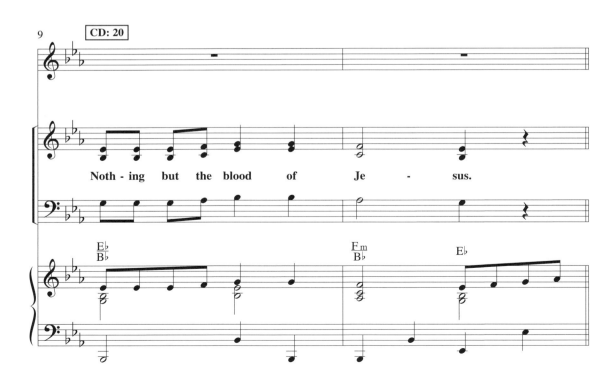

38

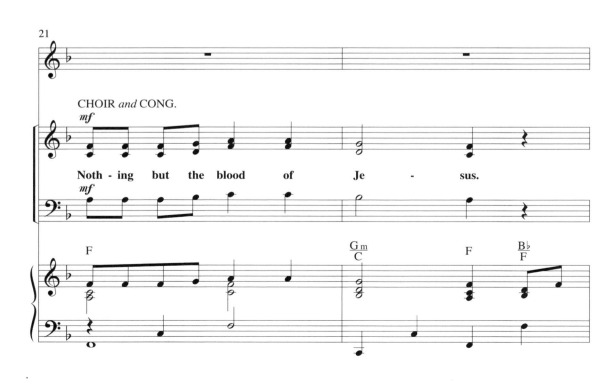

For my cleans - ing this my plea–

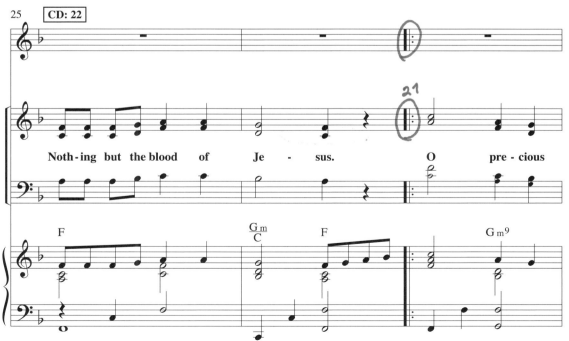

Noth-ing but the blood of Je - sus. O pre - cious

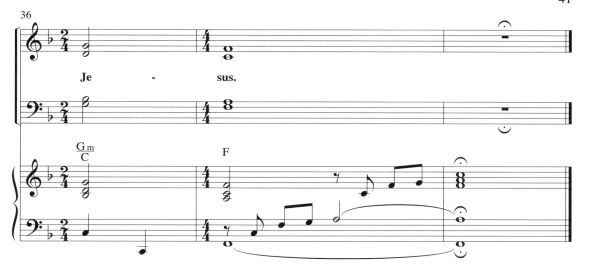

WORSHIP LEADER *(without music)*: The blood of Jesus is powerful. It cleanses our hearts, it covers our sin. It is said that Jesus' blood can even set captives free. This is one man's story about the power of the blood of Christ.

STORYTELLER *(or Worship Leader)*: His tombstone reads, "John Newton . . . once an infidel . . . was, by the rich mercy of our Lord and Savior Jesus Christ, preserved, restored, pardoned . . . "

Yes, this is the epitaph of the well-known songwriter and passionate preacher, John Newton, who had spent most of his life as the captain of slave ships that set sail from his homeland, England. He held others captive, but he had become a slave himself to his own sin.

Once on a voyage, this hard-hearted slave trader found himself in the middle of a violent storm. Out of memory of his departed mother's teachings, he cried, "Lord, have mercy upon us." After the storm had passed, John realized that God's grace had begun its work on him.

It was May 10th, 1748. After that day, slave ship captain, John Newton, began his eternal voyage as a child of God. *(Music begins, Storyteller pauses)* Years later he penned the most beloved and powerful hymn ever written.

WORSHIP LEADER: Sing it with me.

Amazing Grace

with
Amazing Grace–My Chains Are Gone
Grace Flows Down

JOHN NEWTON

Virginia Harmony, 1831
Arr. by Dennis Allen

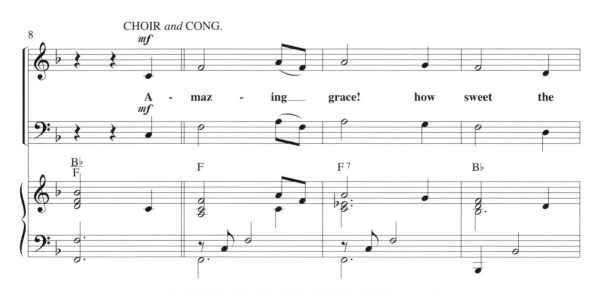

Arr. © 2007 by Pilot Point Music (ASCAP). All rights reserved.
Administered by The Copyright Company, PO Box 128139, Nashville, TN 37212-8139.

PLEASE NOTE: Copying of this product is NOT covered by CCLI licenses. For CCLI information call 1-800-234-2446.

44

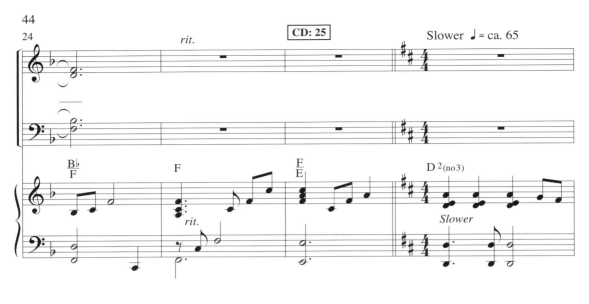

CD: 25

*"Amazing Grace–My Chains Are Gone"

1st time: SOLO – George
2nd time: CHOIR unis.

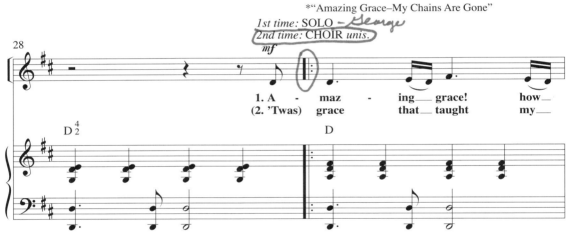

1. A - maz - ing grace! how
(2. 'Twas) grace that taught my

sweet the sound That saved a wretch like
heart to fear, And grace my fears re -

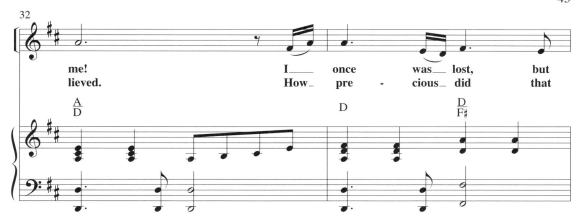

me! / lieved.
I____ once was____ lost, but / How____ pre - cious____ did that

CD: 26 *1st time*
CD: 28 *2nd time*

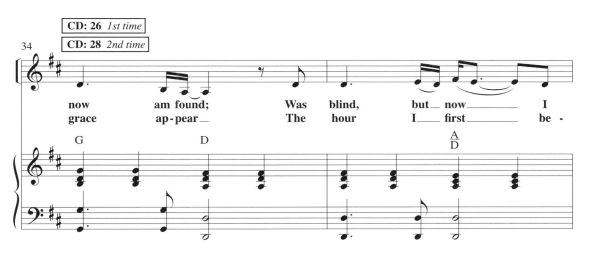

now____ am found; / grace ap-pear____
Was blind, but____ now_____ I / The hour I____ first_____ be -

1st time: SOLO *continues or opt. Choir unis.*
2nd time: CHOIR *parts*

see. / lieved!
My chains are gone,_____ I've been set____

38

free,   My God, my   Sav - ior____ has ran - somed____

D/F#   G/B

40

me;   And like   a   flood_____   His mer - cy

D/A   D/F#   G

42   **CD: 29** *2nd time*

reigns,   Un - end - ing   love,   a - maz - ing

D/F#   E m7   G/A

48

nailed_____ to_____ the tree,_____

CD: 31

As grace___ flows down_____ and cov - ers___ me.

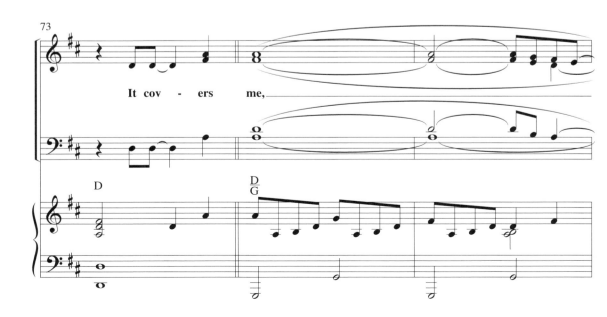

It cov - ers_____ me,_____

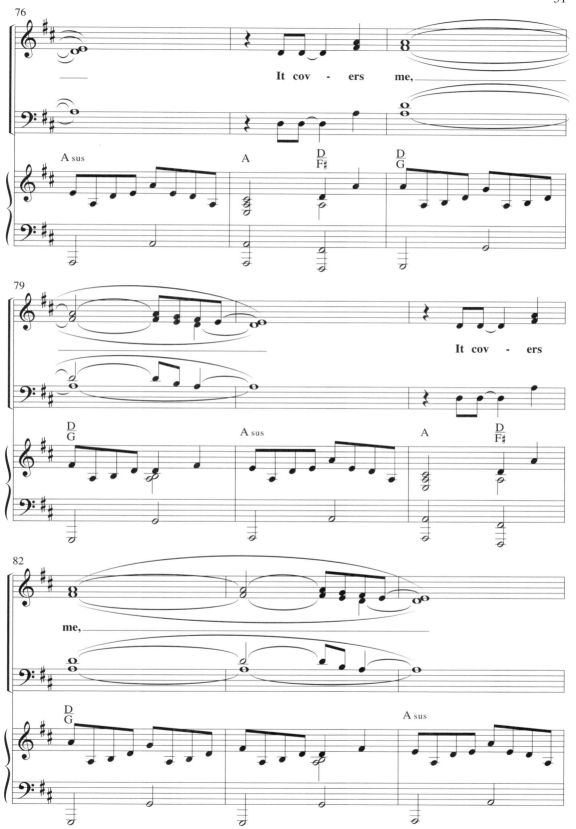

52

STORYTELLER *(or Worship Leader) (without music)*: It was 1945
and a German pastor, teacher, musician and author named Dietrich
Bonhoeffer was himself in chains. Unlike John Newton, Dietrich's
chains were real. The Nazis had held him in concentration camps
for two years and not just because he spoke out against their evil
regime. It was because he would not be silent about what Jesus
had done for him.

On April 9th, Dietrich Bonhoeffer went to the gallows and was
hanged with this thought on his mind: "[Following Christ] is costly
because it costs a man his life, and it is grace because it gives a
man the only true life."

He traded his physical freedom for the freedom in Christ.

(Music begins)

Amazing Grace–My Chains Are Gone
Reprise 1

JOHN NEWTON, CHRIS TOMLIN
and LOUIE GIGLIO

Virginia Harmony, 1831, CHRIS TOMLIN
and LOUIE GIGLIO
Arr. by Dennis Allen

54

The Power of the Cross

Words and Music by
KEITH GETTY and
STUART TOWNEND
Arr. by Dennis Allen

1. O to see the dawn of the dark - est day,
2. O to see the pain writ - ten on Your face

Christ on the road to Cal - va - ry;
bear - ing the awe - some weight of sin;

LADIES *unis.*, *tenderly*

Now the day - light flees,

now the ground be-neath quakes as its mak - er

bows His head;

CHOIR *with strength*

Cur - tain torn in two,

love. This the pow'r of the cross Son of God slain for us; What a life, what a cost, we stand for-giv-en at the cross, We

stand for-giv-en at___ the cross, We stand for-giv-en

at___ the cross.___

WORSHIP LEADER *(without music)*: Jesus said, ". . . everyone is a slave to sin. A slave has no place in the family, but a [child] belongs to it forever. So if the Son [of God] sets you free, you will be free indeed." *(John 8:34-36 NIV para)*

What a statement! What a promise!

Jesus' sacrifice gave us all the opportunity to be God's sons, daughters . . . heirs instead of slaves. So no matter what chains may bind us, be they real, imagined, self-imposed or forced upon us, Christ's blood has power over them all.

Let's remember and celebrate today the freedom we have because of the cleansing blood and broken body of Christ. *(Music begins)*

Communion

with

Jesus Paid It All

Words and Music by
BRAD AVERY, DAVID CARR,
MAC POWELL, MARK LEE
and TAI ANDERSON
Arr. by Dennis Allen

We hun-ger and thirst for Your love,

and Your righ-teous - ness. We long for Your

pres - ence here, Lord, be with us a -

CD: 46

72

WORSHIP LEADER *(without music)*: At the cross, by Jesus' blood, the power of sin was broken. But the victory was not quite complete. Not yet. It would be finished, however, before three days had passed. *(Music begins)*

Jesus Paid it all
page 102

See What a Morning

(Resurrection Hymn)

Words and Music by
KEITH GETTY and
STUART TOWNEND
Arr. by Dennis Allen

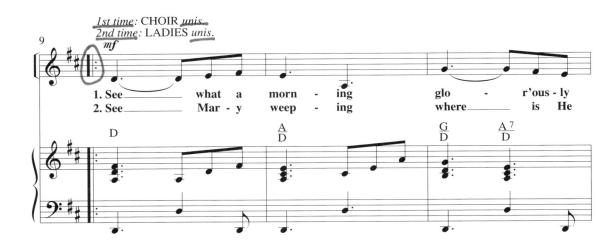

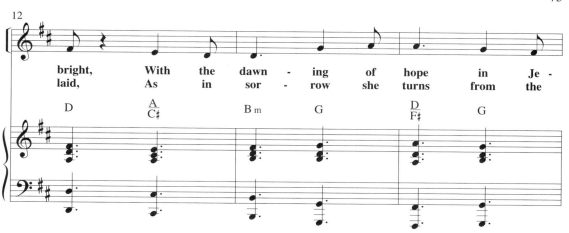

bright, With the dawn - ing of hope in Je -
laid, As in sor - row she turns in from the

D   A/C♯   B m   G   D/F♯   G

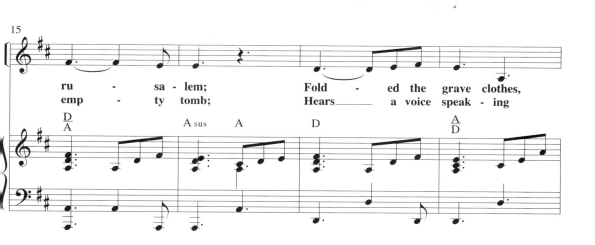

ru - sa - lem; Fold - ed the grave clothes,
emp - ty tomb; Hears_____ a voice speak - ing

D/A   A sus   A   D   A/D

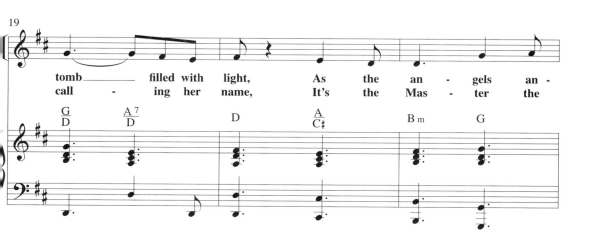

tomb_____ filled with light, As the an - gels an -
call - ing her name, It's the Mas - ter the

G/D   A 7/D   D   A/C♯   B m   G

CD: 50 *1st time*

CD: 52 *2nd time*

nounce Christ is ris - en.
Lord raised to life _____ a - gain.

Parts both times

(1.) See God's sal - va - tion
(2.) The voice that spans the

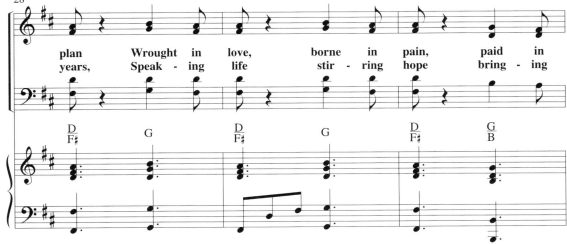

plan Wrought in love, borne in pain, paid in
years, Speak - ing life stir - ring hope bring - ing

78

WORSHIP LEADER *(without music)*: How can we NOT sing about that? How can we not shout it from the rooftops? How can we not praise God today . . . for His love . . . for His mercy . . . for the gift of His Son as a blood sacrifice?

We can never repay Him so there's no need trying. *(Music begins)* All we can do is worship Him . . . praise Him . . . honor Him.

My Heart Is Filled

Words and Music by
KEITH GETTY and
STUART TOWNEND
Arr. by Dennis Allen

light; And— wrote His law of righ-teous-ness with
take; Sus - tain - ing me with arms of love and

pow'r up - on my heart.
crown - ing me with

2. My—

(to pg. 84, meas. 5)

Amazing Grace–My Chains Are Gone

Reprise 2

with

How Can I Keep from Singing

Reprise

JOHN NEWTON, CHRIS TOMLIN
and LOUIE GIGLIO

Virginia Harmony, 1831, CHRIS TOMLIN
and LOUIE GIGLIO
Arr. by Dennis Allen

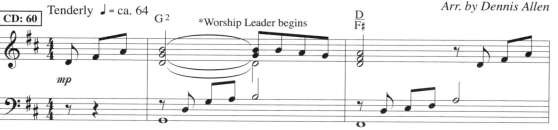

*WORSHIP LEADER: Do you wear some kind of chains today? Are they chains of addiction, chains of anger, chains of past failures? Remember Jesus died . . . and rose again to break those chains. All you have to do is surrender. I know that's hard to do. It's not an easy thing to give up power over our own lives. But that's the only way to truly break free. It is true freedom by surrender.

Can we sing that song again?

flood _____ His mer - cy reigns, Un- end - ing

love, a - maz - ing grace.

rit.

Brightly, in two ♩. = ca. 69

CD: 61

Brightly, in two

rit.

*"How Can I Keep from Singing"

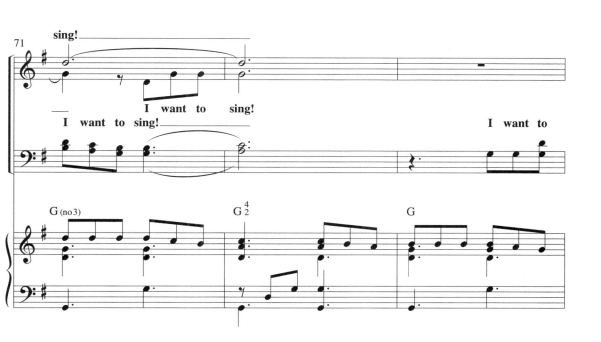

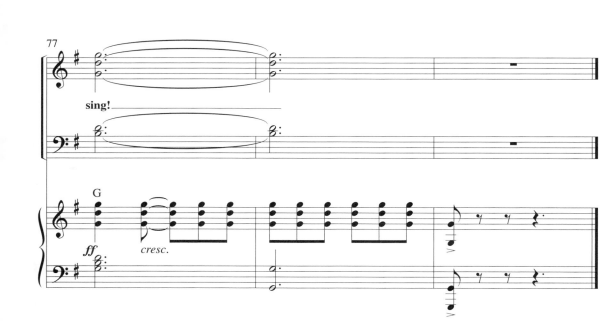

Production Notes

Worship Experience

This musical was designed as an Easter worship experience. That is one of the reasons we have included some familiar songs and hymns that the congregation can join in singing. Please feel free to engage the audience any time.

Narrator

The "Narrator" has been called the "Worship Leader" in the script. The words assigned to this character can be divided up among more than one worship leader (the music minister, the worship pastor, the pastor, etc.) or other narrators.

Storytellers

The stories of John Newton and Dietrich Bonhoeffer may be presented by the same worship leaders you choose for narrators. However, these two stories can be told (preferably from memory) by others you choose to communicate them. Some members of the choir may be asked to serve in this capacity.

Communion Service

Following the song "Communion", you may want to include a Lord's Supper/ Communion service with your congregation. Accompaniment tracks have been provided in sequence on the accompaniment CD (tracks 47 and 48). The printed music for this service has also been provided at the back of this book if you wish to use "live" players. Feel free to adapt this to your needs.

"Jesus Paid It All" may be sung or played in the distribution of the "bread." "At the Cross" may be used to distribute the "cup." Again, feel free to adapt this to your needs.

Here are some scripture passages that may be spoken by a worship leader as he or she presents the elements of the communion service:

Matthew 26:17-28   1 Corinthians 11:23-26

Whether the optional communion service is used, the song "Communion" with "Jesus Paid It All" still works in the musical as a choir or congregational song.

Jesus Paid It All

ELVINA M. HALL

JOHN T. GRAPE

to page 14

At the Cross

ISAAC WATTS and
RALPH E. HUDSON

RALPH E. HUDSON

Optional **CD: 48**

1. A - las! and did my Sav - ior bleed, And
2. Was it for crimes that I have done He
3. Well might the sun in dark - ness hide, And
4. Thus might I hide my blush - ing face While
5. But drops of grief can ne'er re - pay The

did my Sov - 'reign die? Would He de - vote that
groaned up - on the tree? A - maz - ing pit - y!
shut His glo - ries in When Christ, the might - y
Cal - v'ry's cross ap - pears, Dis - solve my heart in
debt of love I owe. Here, Lord, I give my -

sa - cred head For sin - ners such as I?
grace un - known! And love be - yond de - gree!
Mak - er, died For man, the crea - ture's, sin.
thank - ful - ness, And melt mine eyes to tears.
self a - way; 'Tis all that I can do.

Refrain

At the cross, at the cross, where I first saw the light, And the

bur - den of my heart rolled a - way, It was there by faith I re -
ceived my sight, And now I am hap - py all the day!